Change the World for Ten Bucks

First published in Great Britain 2004 as **Change the World for a Fiver**
by Short Books Ltd 15 Highbury Terrace, London N5 1UP

This edition published in Australia 2005 by Pilotlight Australia on behalf
of We Are What We Do Ltd and in conjunction with Hardie Grant Publishing
85 High Street Prahran, Victoria 3181, Australia www.hardiegrant.com.au

A CiP record is available for this title from the National Library of Australia

Printed on paper from trees grown in sustainable forests.

3 5 7 9 10 8 6 4 2

Change the World for Ten Bucks

50 actions to change the world and make you feel great

Designed in the UK by Antidote
Creative team: Tim Ashton, Steve Henry, Ken Hoggins, Chris O'Shea, Chris Wigan, David Robinson, Eugenie Harvey and Paul Twivy.

Designed in Australia by Whybin\TBWA
Creative team: Bruce Baldwin, Nerida Simpson, Amy Smith and Michael Syme.
The development of Change The World For Ten Bucks and We Are What We Do in Australia is led by Judith Swales, Ricci Swart and Jane Tewson.

The project has been generously supported by Pacific Brands.

PILOTLIGHT
CREATIVE PHILANTHROPY

Hardie Grant Publishing

we are what we do

We Are What We Do is a project of the UK charity Community Links. Community Links tackles the causes and consequences of social exclusion in east London and shares the local experience with practitioners and policy makers nationwide.

'Change the World For Ten Bucks' has been made possible by the UK bestseller 'Change The World For A Fiver' originally produced by We Are What We Do.

We Are What We Do has worked in partnership with Pilotlight Australia to create 'Change The World For Ten Bucks'.

Pilotlight is a charity committed to inspiring and enabling others to find a new way to make a difference to significant social issues.

We believe in acting local and thinking global.

Everyone who has contributed to the book in the UK and Australia has done so for free. Money raised from the sales of the book will be used to cover the costs of production. This means that the book is worth double, triple, possibly even quadruple the money you've paid for it.

For further information about We Are What We Do, or to make comments or suggestions, please visit www.wearewhatwedo.org

For further information about Community Links, please visit www.community-links.org

For further information about Pilotlight, please visit www.pilotlight.org.au

PILOTLIGHT
CREATIVE PHILANTHROPY

community links

We live in peculiar times. More communications devices than ever before can connect us, yet more people live alone. We want to belong to communities but our cities can be very lonely places.

We buy things – more and more things – with more and more money; but they don't make us happy – life satisfaction was higher during post-war rationing in the 1940s.

The rich are getting richer, but nearly 10% of Australians are shockingly poor. The other 90% experience other kinds of poverty: most of us feel that our lives are missing something.

Membership of political parties and unions continues to decline, but in a crisis such as the Asian Tsunami Australians have shown how they can and will pull together to help their neighbours.

We feel things very deeply and we want to do something, but what?

It was Mahatma Gandhi who said: 'We must be the change we want to see in the world'. In other words, we are what we do.

So why is it so difficult?

Perhaps it is the scale of the problems which induces the state of paralysis. We think we have to leave change to governments or big business even though we also know that we elect governments and that our spending is what creates big business.

Surely the question now is not whether we should act alone but how can we act together.

We Are What We Do is a new kind of movement – a movement with attitude. We are not trying to raise money. We are trying to show the power of a simple shift in attitudes and day-to-day behaviour.

We invite you to be part of a new kind of global community; not of joiners but of independent doers following the same banner and answering the questions that we all want answered.

Who are we? We Are What We Do.

How to use this book.

This is a book of simple, everyday actions we reckon pretty much all of us can do. If you're reading this book, chances are you, or someone you know, has actually done one of the actions already (Action 33 Recycle Your Books or Action 47 Buy a Copy of This Book for a Friend) so you're already on your way!

Each page has an action strip down the right-hand side. This says what the action is.

A number of pages feature references to organisations which can help you perform the actions - for example, Action 26 Give Blood features the website address for the Australian Red Cross Blood Service so you can find your nearest donation centre.

We've included a whole host of related websites in Action 49 Learn More, Do More, at the end of the book which will give you more information about the action and how to do it.

We're not suggesting that either the list of actions or of websites in Action 49 are definitive - but they are a start. We'd love to hear from you, either with suggestions for new actions, or suggestions for other helpful organisations and websites. Please email us at wearewhatwedo@pilotlight.org.au and check out our website to see updated lists of both.

Give someone a kiss they'll remember for the rest of their life.

Take five minutes to learn how to do the kiss of life. Better still, take a couple of days and do a first aid course.

Let's face it, saving someone's life is cool. In fact, it's about as cool as you can possibly get.

And, if you do learn this skill, you might like to know that the person you help is statistically unlikely to be a stranger.

They're much more likely to be a friend or relative.

Imagine saving your best friend's life.

1. Check if breathing.

Illustration: Bruce Baldwin

2. If not breathing, tilt head back, pinch nose and breathe into mouth.

3. Watch for a rise in chest, repeat breath and look for obvious signs of life. Continue breaths, 15 times a minute, until help arrives or the person is breathing.

Call 000 for an ambulance.

Photography: Stuart Crossett.com.au

The 500 year shopping trip.

Every person in Australia uses an average of 300 plastic bags every year.

That's 6 billion bags all together.

A plastic bag can take up to 500 years to decay in landfill.

There is an alternative.

It's called a shopping bag. And all major supermarkets now sell them for just a couple of bucks.

Not only will using one help the planet but your oranges are less likely to burst through the bottom and roll down the footpath.

Illustration: Sholto Walker at illustrationweb.com

When kids ask you to read a story to them, it's because they know something you don't.
They know you'll both feel richer for the experience.

Capture a child's imagination...

Photo: Kevin Anthony Horgan / Getty Images

Change a light bulb and see what you can save.

An energy-saving light bulb might not seem cheap but over its lifetime it could save up to 75% of electricity consumption and a lot more besides. Like the planet for example.

Photo: Judy Lambert / Getty Images

It takes half as many muscles to smile as it does to frown.

And it makes you and others feel twice as good.

Illustration: Andrew Selby at illustrationweb.com

A bus carries the same number of people as 50 cars. And it's going there anyway.

Photography: Christopher Howe at bluefish.com.au

Plants are amazing things. They take in stuff we don't like (carbon dioxide) and pump out stuff we do (oxygen). But we get rid of these amazing things astonishingly quickly. We're losing 2000 trees a minute in rainforests around the world.

Planting a tree or a native bush will not only help redress the balance, it'll also encourage native wildlife back to the area. Each tree will provide oxygen for 2 people for the rest of their lives.

And many councils even offer native seeds for free. Can you dig it?

Help fill a hole in our oxygen supply.

Save water. Have fun. Just get out before everything becomes wrinkled.

Illustration: Andy Holmes at Three Blind Mice

HAVE A BATH WITH SOMEONE YOU LOVE

ACTION 08

Respect your elders.

Apache. Cherokee. Comanche. Mohican. Sioux. Recognise them? Of course you do; they're Native American tribes.

Now can you name five Australian Aboriginal Nations? Not so easy, huh?

This is all the more surprising when you discover that there are over 260 different Aboriginal Nations in Australia – each with its own language and culture.

As a first step, discover the name of the traditional owners of your capital city. Done that? Learn the names of some other groups. Or better still, learn something about them.

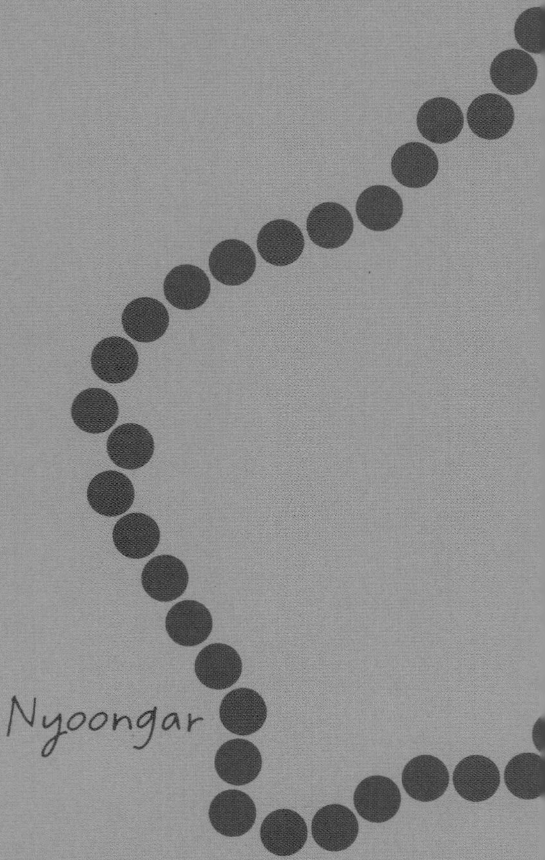

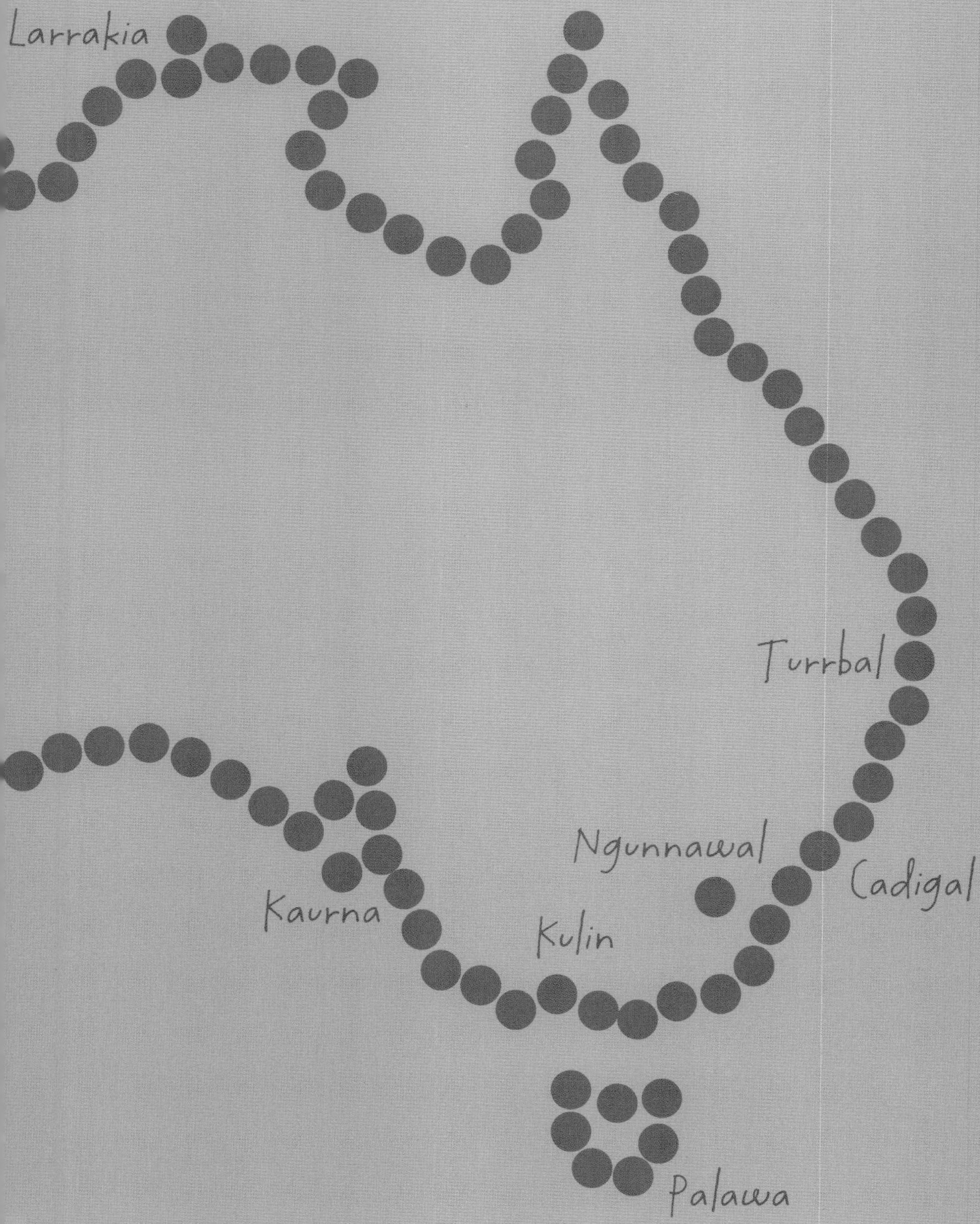
Larrakia
Turrbal
Ngunnawal
Cadigal
Kaurna
Kulin
Palawa

Spot the difference.

If you turn your heating thermostat down by one degree, you'll save 15% on your bill. Turn it down another degree and you'll save another 15%.

The same is true for air conditioning. Set the thermostat one degree higher than usual and save yet another 15%.

That'll give you something extra to give to charity (see Action 16).

Photo: John Lamb / Getty Images

10
15
20
25
30

10
15
20
25
30

Illustration: Willie Ryan at illustrationweb.com

Walk more.

Obesity is turning into a massive problem in the developed world.

One suggestion from doctors is to do something simple such as walking up a couple of flights of stairs every day.

Although, if you are obese, you're not going to want to do this because inevitably you'll sweat a lot. Which will draw attention to the very thing you're trying to deal with.

So much for doctors.

But try walking as much as you can.

If that's only from the sweets trolley to the cheese board and back again – well, that's a starter.

Well, no it isn't – it's a dessert. But you get the idea.

Photo: Bryan Mullenmix / Getty Images

A TV that's on standby is still using a lot of electricity.

And a video recorder on standby uses almost as much electricity as one playing a tape.

Switching that little 'standby' light from green to red doesn't actually do you, or the planet, much good.

It's still costing you money and wasting energy.

Illustration: Tim Ashton / Antidote

Make sure you phone back.

There are an estimated 10 million unused mobile phones just lying around homes and offices in Australia. On top of this, we're buying nearly 4 million new mobiles a year. That's a hell of a lot of annoying ringtones.

Even worse, if these phones are dumped in landfill, poisonous substances contained in the phones can seep into groundwater, contaminate the soil and enter the food chain.

So despite your strong desire to grab the Flip Up 2200 that's ringing next to you in the cinema and chuck it in the bin, resist.

The least irritating thing about your mobile should be what use it can be put to after its death.

Mobile phones can be recycled at most phone retailers.

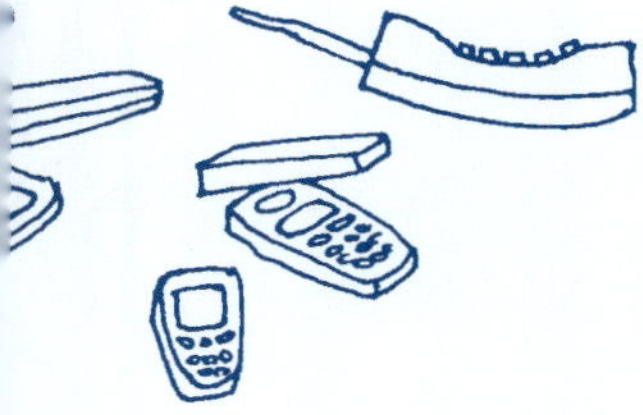

Photography: Carlos Alcaide at heavenpictures.com

Talk to young people
They know
cool stuff

After you've died, let your heart beat inside someone else's chest.

Let your liver live, after you've passed on.

Even your eyes could give someone else a new look.

Australia's organ donor rate of just 10.4% is the second lowest in the developed world. At any given time, there are almost 2000 people in Australia on organ transplant waiting lists. 15% of them will die waiting.

To make sure your wishes are carried out, you need to do two things:

Firstly, tell your next of kin about your wishes and ask them about theirs.

Secondly, register on line at www.hic.gov.au

So next time you're surfing the net – make sure you 'save' before you log off.

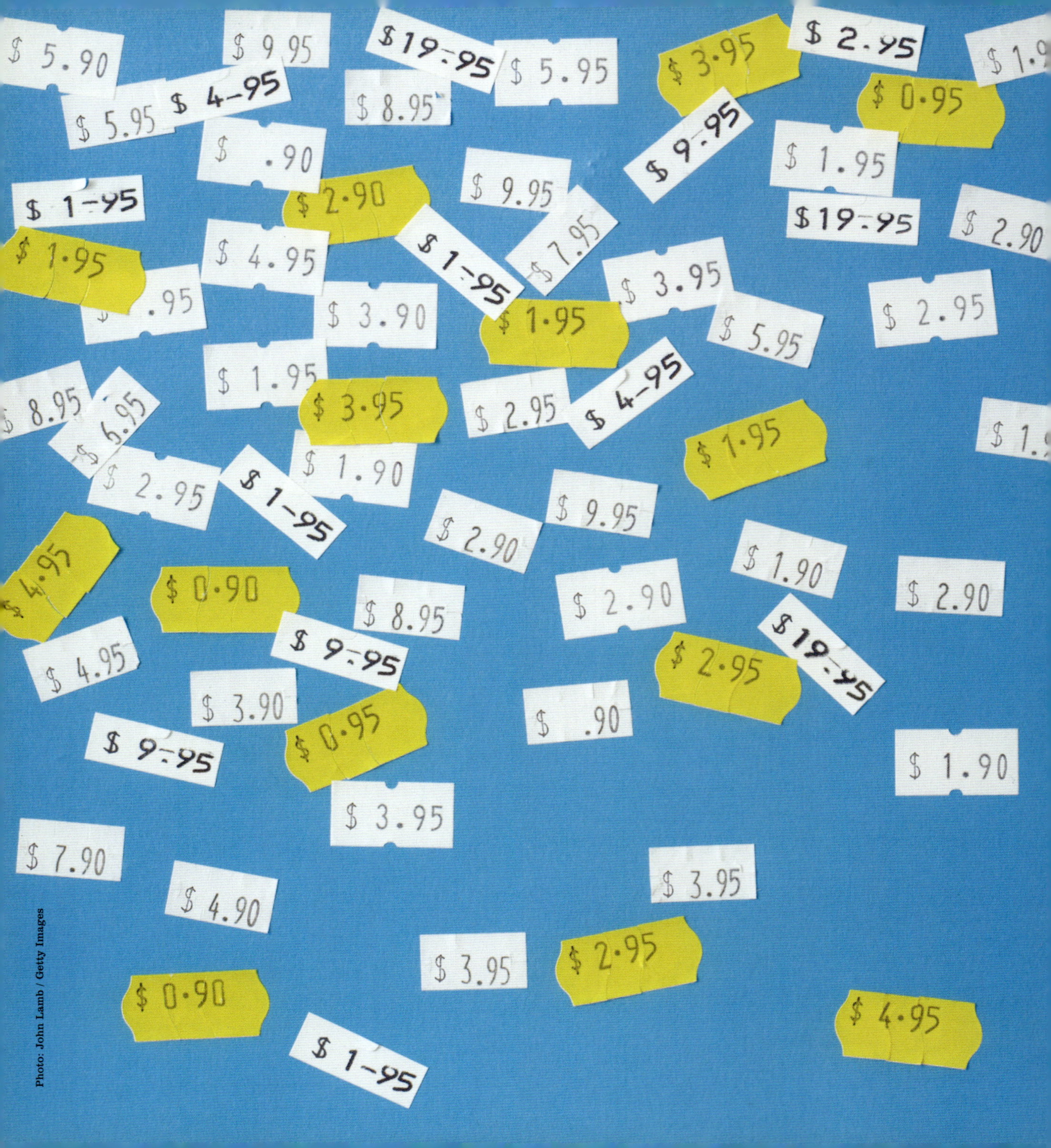

Photo: John Lamb / Getty Images

Lose money instantly.

There's always loose change – and there are always charity tins.

It's a match made in heaven – like ham and eggs, Kath and Kim, or Delta and... well, Delta and New Idea.

If we all put our loose change into charity tins, the world would be a lot better off.

So the next time your change is just a coin or two, look around for a charity tin.

After all, 5 cents per person, per week, adds up to $52 million per year.

One word of warning, though. If the golden retriever sitting outside the shop doesn't have a slot in his head, don't try putting your coins in. He won't appreciate it.

Photo: Getty Images

Rearrange your pictures.

Make a cocktail.

File.

Write a song.

Apply make-up.

Swim in a dam.

Wear gold.

Revert to childhood.

Stay up all night.

Change your hair colour.

Turn left instead of right.

Streak.

Massage someone.

Dust.

Shave something off.

	Arabic	Chinese (Mandarin)	Italian	Aboriginal (Gunnai)
Hello	Salaamu Alaikum (Peace Be Upon You)	Nee How	Buongiorno	Wunman Njin
Goodbye	Salaamu Alaikum (Peace Be Upon You)	Zai Jien	Arrivederci	Yarrabee
Please	Min Fadlik	Ching	Per favore	Kanitba
Thank you	Shukran	Share Share	Grazie	Kanitba
Can I help?	Mumkin sa 'adak?	Wo nung bung ni ma?	Posso aiutare?	Njinde bow?
Would you like a cup of tea?	Hal turid finjan shai? (turidi - for female)	Ni yow bu yow yi bay cha?	Vorrebbe una tazza di té?	Glookban mu

Maori

Tena koe

Haere rä

Koa

Nga mihi nui ki koe

Maaku koe i whina?

He kapu ti mou?

Ma yumkin an as 'ad?

Yes, you can help actually.

Just by learning a few words in a foreign language, it's amazing how much genuine warmth you can generate.

It's not something we Aussies tend to do well, but it's a lot easier than you think.

For instance, in Arabic the word for 'hello' is the same as the word for 'goodbye'.

Which is a lovely sentiment, although it could make telephone calls rather confusing.

'... So the dog said...'

Illustration: Gray Jolliffe at illustrationweb.com

Make people laugh at you.

Learn at least one good joke.

Laughing tones your stomach, lowers your blood pressure, and makes you healthier. It's scientifically proven.

Even the concentration of salivary immunoglobulin A is raised by laughing, and this guards our respiratory tract from infectious organisms.

But that in itself isn't very funny.

Unlike the story about the chicken that walks into a library, goes up to the desk and says, "Bok". The librarian hands it a book and it walks out. A few minutes later, it's back and says, "Bok, bok". The librarian hands it two books. A few minutes it's back again, "Bok, bok, bok". This time the librarian follows it as it walks down the street, into a park, and over to a frog sitting in a pond. As the chicken holds up each of the books the frog says, "Readit, readit, readit."

Photo: Getty Images

TURN OFF UNNECESSARY LIGHTS

ACTION 20

All those offices with lights
burning bright at night.

Are they really all full of
people working late?

Or is it some cock-eyed theory of
aesthetics which says that lighting
an empty space is beautiful?

Ivory was considered beautiful once.

Fur was considered beautiful once.

Illustration: Nick Diggory at nickdiggory.com

Make sure your super fund has the same values as you.

Unless you check that your superannuation is ethically invested, chances are that you're supporting companies with poor human rights and environmental records.

Now, this is a complicated area, and even if you're just thinking about your super, you deserve some kind of medal.

So, to make this as simple as possible – just ask your superannuation provider one question: 'Can you ensure that my investments don't harm the planet or hurt my fellow man?'

If we all did that, super providers would soon take notice.

But don't get caught up in a longer conversation, unless you're desperate for company.

As Woody Allen once said, anybody who wants to know the definition of eternity should try spending an evening talking to a life insurance salesman.

Have

David Davis, in 1788, left his wife five shillings to 'enable her to get drunk for the last time at my expense'.

Juan Potomachi, in 1955, left $70,000 to the Teatro Dramatico Theatre provided his skull could be used in Hamlet.

to make

In 1990 a lady left $250,000 to the King George Hospital for the 'expansion, improvement and maintenance of its lavatories'.

Dentist Philip Grundy, in 1974, left dental nurse Amelia White $450,000 on condition that she didn't go out with men or wear make-up or jewellery for five years.

Do It Yourself Will Kits are available from Post Offices as well as online (Action 49). For helpful advice on making a will, visit moneymanager.smh.com.au/tools/factsheet/will_making.html
And then you can make sure that your goodies don't go to the baddies.

the will

Samuel Bratt, whose wife would not let him smoke, left her, in 1960, a million dollars on condition that she smoked five cigars a day.

a will.

In 1926, Charles Vance Millar, a wealthy Toronto lawyer, bequeathed his estate to whichever woman gave birth to the most babies in the ten-year period following his death.

Hensley Nankivell requested, in 1987, that any relative wanting to benefit from his million dollar estate must first train as an airline pilot.

Research has shown that children who have meals with their parents are much less likely to suffer from anxiety or stress disorders.

So why not try chatting to each other?

George Bush Snr said that America needed more families like the Waltons, and less like the Simpsons.

A very bad idea, as it happens – after all, when was the last time you laughed at the Waltons?

But if you notice, even the Simpsons like to eat together.

Photo: John Lamb / Getty Images

Minimise pollution. No ifs or butts.

Do we still need to remind people not to toss their butts away?

Over 9 billion butts are thrown away each year in New South Wales alone. If laid end to end they'd circle the globe four and a half times.

Not only do they leach toxins into the soil and waterways but they just make the whole country look messy.

So do the right thing and don't turn Australia into an ashtray.

Don't let your old pants
Sit 'round the house all day,
Give them to an op shop,
Send them out to play.

Illustration: Bruce Baldwin.

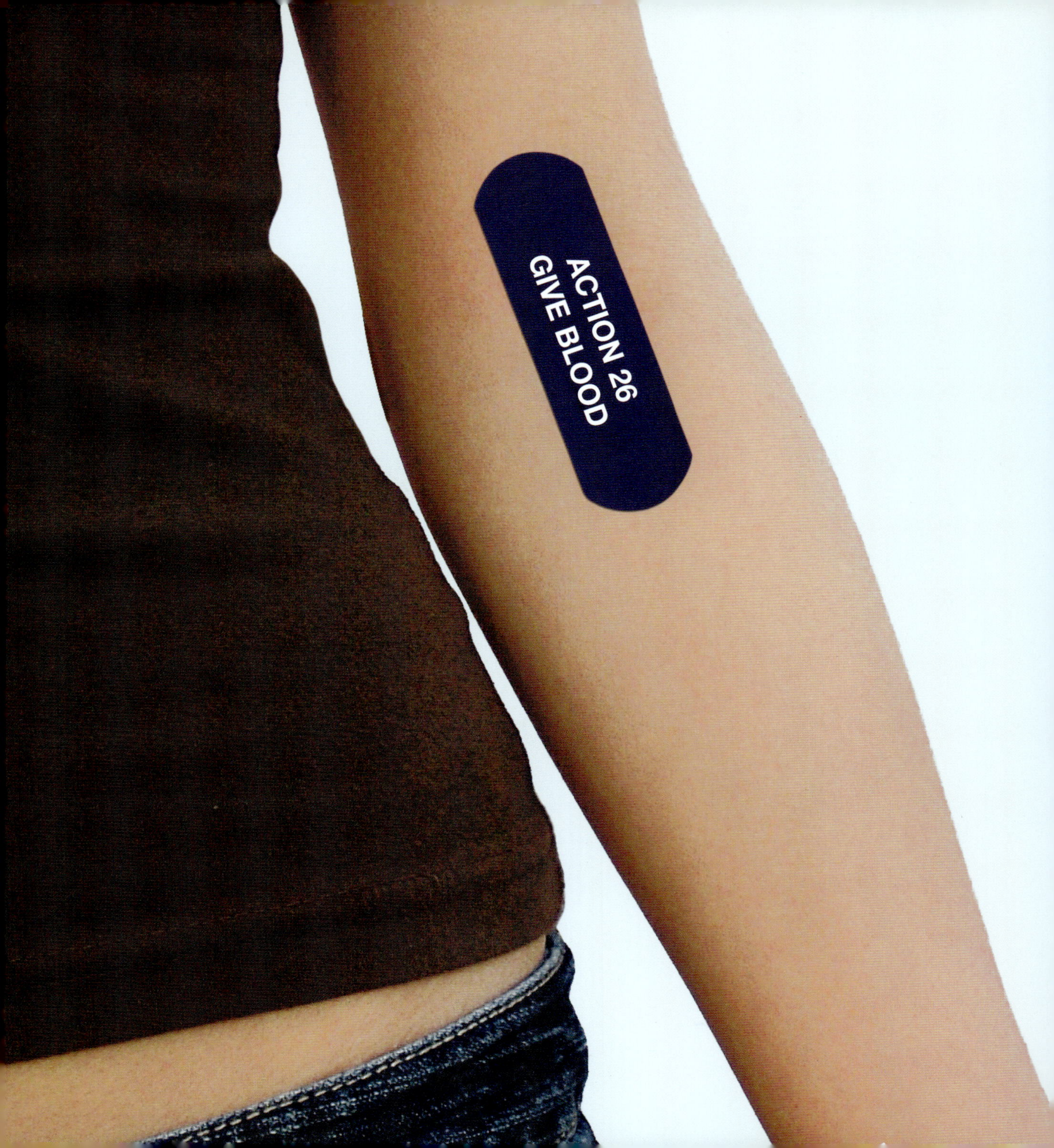
ACTION 26
GIVE BLOOD

The medical side-effects of giving blood:
1. Slight euphoria
2. Puffed up chest
3. Broad smile

One in three Australians will need blood in their lifetime, yet only one in thirty currently donates.

Who would have thought that something so easy to do could have such profound effects? Your one donation could help to save up to three people's lives.

Bloody fantastic.

To make an appointment, call 13 14 95 or visit www.donateblood.com.au

Illustration: Paul Daviz at Three Blind Mice

The art of reverse haggling.

Confuse the wonderful people who work in op shops. Pay them more than they bargained for. Oh, and do the same for people who sell **The Big Issue**.

“Be the change you want to see in the world.”

Mahatma Gandhi

SEIZE THE MOMENT

ACTION 28

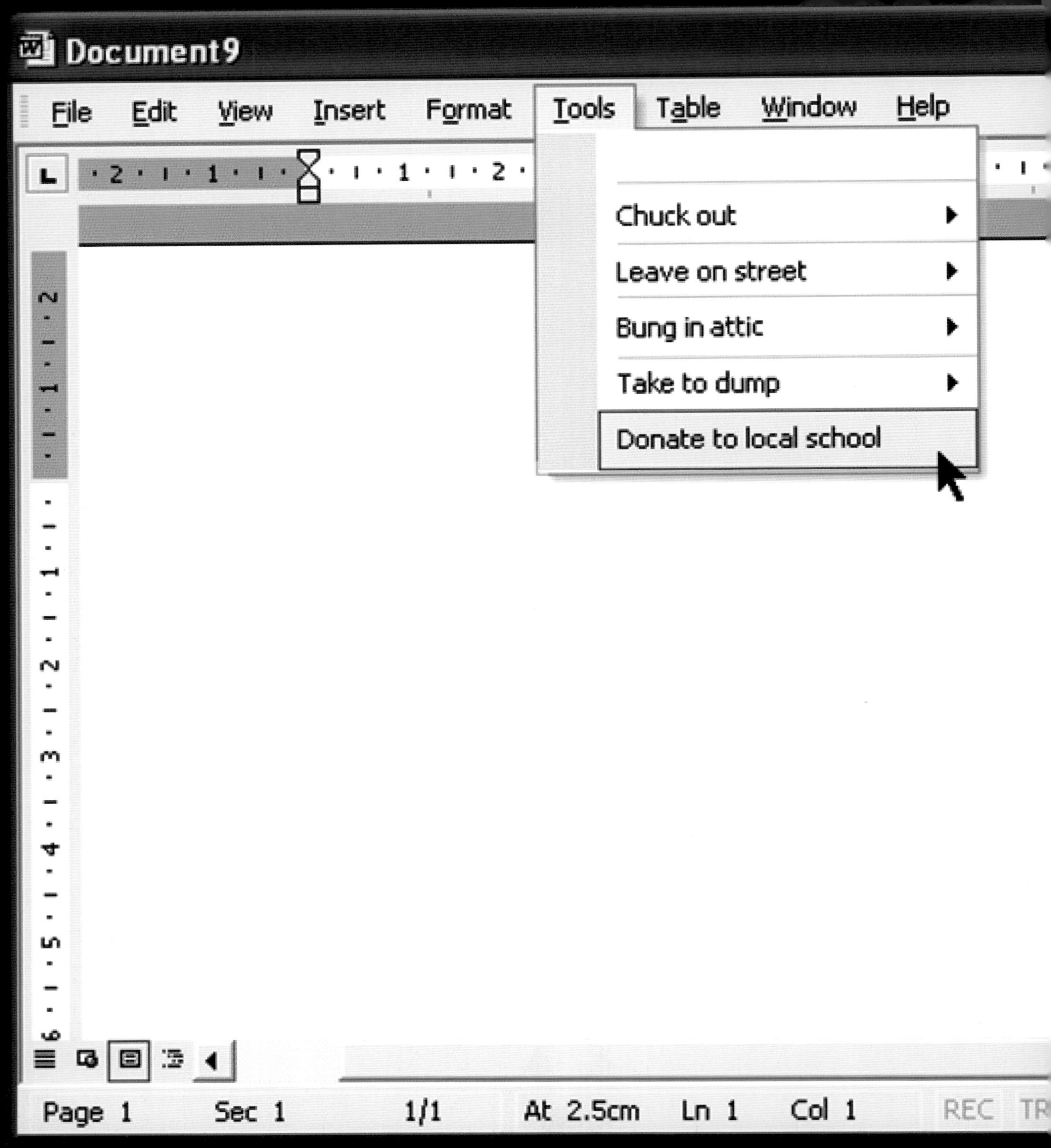
Document9
File
Edit
View
Insert
Format
Tools
Table
Window
Help
Chuck out
Leave on street
Bung in attic
Take to dump
Donate to local school
Page 1
Sec 1
1/1
At 2.5cm
Ln 1
Col 1
REC

What we say about mobile phones in Action 13 applies equally to computers. Except that computers are slightly heavier to carry down the street.

So, if you've got a computer you don't need anymore, contact any of the websites mentioned in Action 49, and they'll help you get it to someone who can make good use of it here or abroad.

Imagine the joy a seven year old in the developing world would feel if they could play with the mightiest thing ever invented.

The thing you currently use to play 'Solitaire' and visit dating sites.

Food Styling: Teresa Cutter. Photography: Paul Cutter

Cook up a great relationship.

Next time you need to buy
a friend a present, don't.
Make them one instead.

Anzac Biscuits

1 cup plain flour

1 cup rolled oats (regular oatmeal) uncooked

1 cup desiccated coconut

1 cup brown sugar

1/2 cup butter

2 tbsp golden syrup (or honey)

1 tsp bicarbonate of soda

2 tbsp boiling water

Combine the flour (sifted), oats, coconut and sugar in a bowl.

Melt the butter and golden syrup (or honey) in a saucepan over a low heat.

Mix the bicarbonate of soda with the water and add to the butter and golden syrup.

Pour the liquids into the dry ingredients and mix well.

Spoon dollops of mixture, about the size of a walnut shell, onto a greased tin, leaving as much space again between dollops to allow for spreading.

Bake in a moderate oven, 180C / 350F, for 15-20 minutes.

Cool on a wire rack and seal in airtight containers.

Give away immediately.

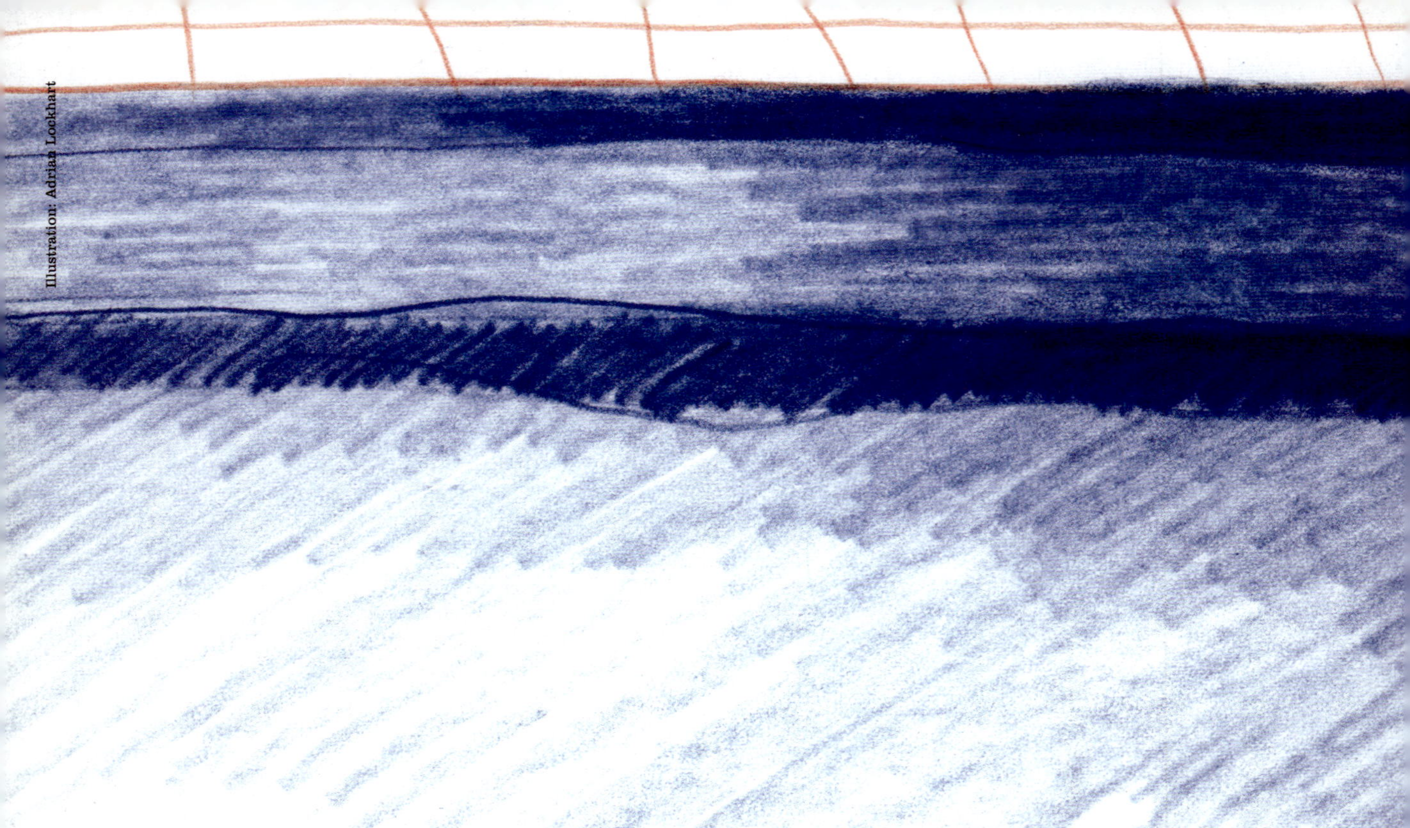

Illustration: Adrian Lockhart

Brush up on your water savings.

Most people leave the tap running while brushing their teeth.

This wastes up to 9 litres of water a minute or 26,000 litres of water per family, per year.

This means your street alone could fill an Olympic sized swimming pool each year.

This wastes huge amounts of water and is a bit stupid – it's like having the toilet flush the whole time you're on it.

So why not turn off the tap while you clean your teeth?

(We bet this is one of the actions you don't forget from this book. For some reason, it seems to strike a chord with everyone.)

TURN OFF THE TAP WHILE BRUSHING YOUR TEETH

ACTION 31

MEND IT
RATHER
THAN
CAUTION
Replace IT

Glue it.

Screw it.

Tie it up.

Tape it down.

Darn it.

Oil it.

Sand it off.

Sew it back on.

Everytime you repair something, you help the world's resources last a little bit longer. And you might just help

Save it.

Rob

John

Sinem

Tomy

Nyto L

Michael

Sara D

Alex F

Kim Van

Margot

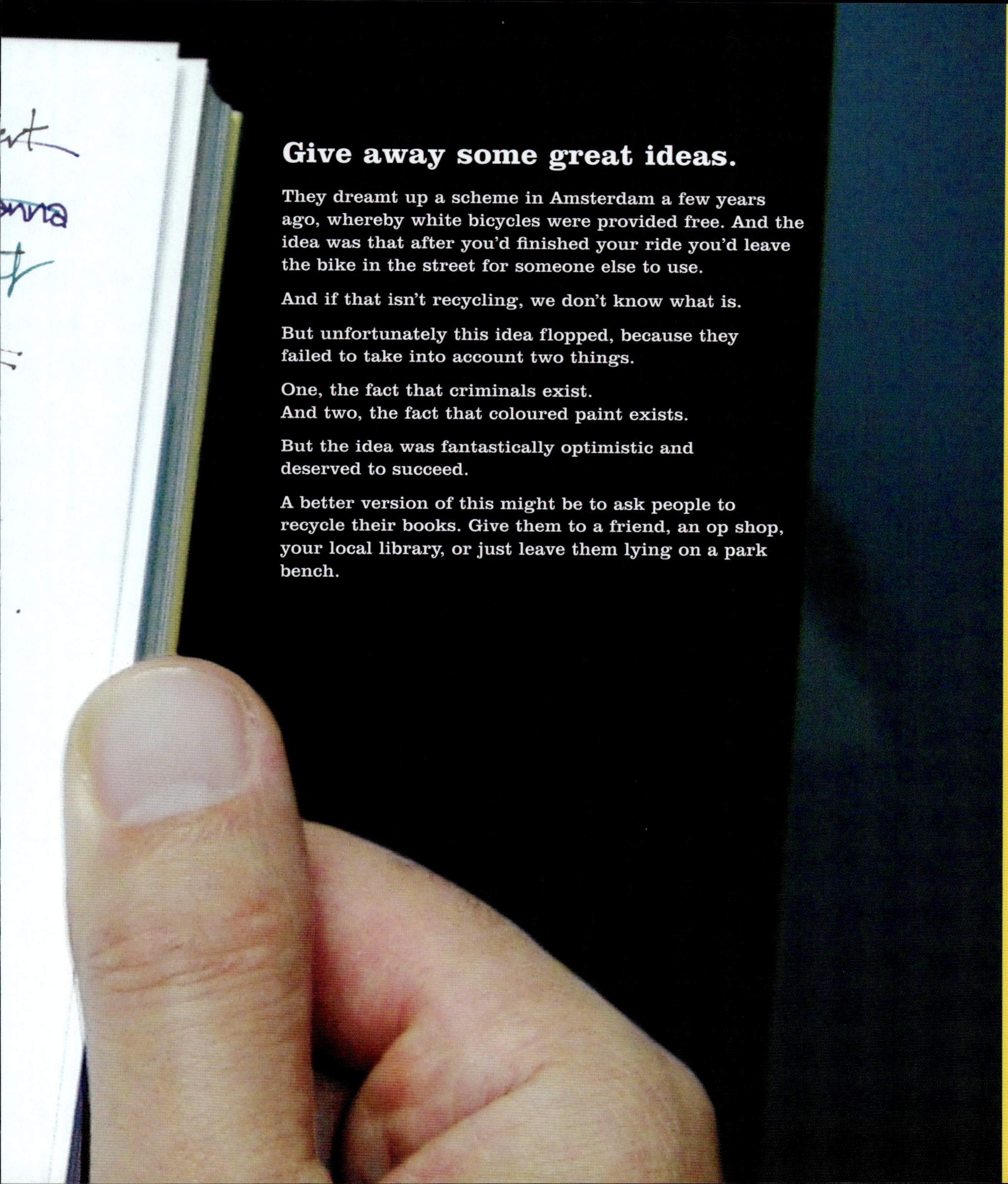

Give away some great ideas.

They dreamt up a scheme in Amsterdam a few years ago, whereby white bicycles were provided free. And the idea was that after you'd finished your ride you'd leave the bike in the street for someone else to use.

And if that isn't recycling, we don't know what is.

But unfortunately this idea flopped, because they failed to take into account two things.

One, the fact that criminals exist.
And two, the fact that coloured paint exists.

But the idea was fantastically optimistic and deserved to succeed.

A better version of this might be to ask people to recycle their books. Give them to a friend, an op shop, your local library, or just leave them lying on a park bench.

A short cut to friendship.

This action isn't just about mowing lawns. It's about finding simple ways to help people in your community. Collect a neighbour's mail while they're on holiday. Take an elderly person's dog for a walk. Help someone by carrying their shopping. They'll be grateful. You'll feel great.

Illustration: Bob Shields.

OFFER TO MOW YOUR NEIGHBOUR'S LAWN

ACTION 34

Say ‘thanks a heap’ to someone who inspired you.

Thanks
Thanks Thanks Thanks Thanks
ACTION 35
WRITE TO SOMEONE WHO INSPIRED YOU

Don't j
somet
Sit the

Illustration: Bob Shields.

Right now, around 1 million Australian adults and 100,000 young people are living with depression.

On average, 1 in 5 people will experience depression at some point in their lives.

But there are lots of little things we can all do to make the world a less depressing place.

Like… just listening. It's a real art, actually – and not as easy as it sounds.

Listen to someone, don't make any comments, don't try to solve their problems. Just listen.

ust do
hing.
re.

Only fill the kettle with the water you need.

If everybody did this, we could save enough electricity to run all the street lighting in the whole country.

Apparently.

Whoever worked that statistic out, should get out more. (Or maybe they can't, because the lights in their street don't work.)

Photo: John Lamb / Getty Images

DON'T OVERFILL YOUR KETTLE

ACTION 37

Illustration: Andy Hammond at illustrationweb.com

Beat road rage.

Just about every driver has been the victim of road rage.

Here's an idea. When you're next at a junction, let a car out ahead of you – but only if it's less cool than your own car.

If we all did that, the world would be a better place.

And if someone driving a Leyland P76 lets you out first, don't worry about it.

It's not personal.

Photo: Nick Walker / Oliver Davies

We're
CLOSED
So sorry, hope you don't need anything too urgent.
The thing is, not enough of you have been coming to see us recently. We think it might have something to do with the big shop that's opened up down the road.
We've loved being here but just can't afford to stay open any more.
See you.

www.

abbasite.com
anca.org.au (Australian National Choral Association)
abf.com.au (Bridge Federation)
auschess.org.au
aflkidszone.com.au
amnesty.org.au
archery.org.au
australiansreunited.com.au
amra.asn.au (Australian Model Railway Association)
ballroomdancing.com.au
birdsaustralia.com.au
bushwalkingaustralia.org
bowls-aust.com.au
bicycles.net.au
canoe.org.au
cricket.com.au
decoupage.com.au
dinosaursociety.com
earthwatch.org/australia
foe.org.au (Friends of the Earth)
fola.org.au (Friend of Libraries Australia)
football.com.au
fruitflycircus.com.au
greenweb.com.au (Gardening Club)
goodcompany.com.au
greenpeace.org.au
guidesaus.org.au
hockey.org.au
judoaustralia.com.au
jupitermining.com
keepaustraliabeautiful.org.au
maketradefair.com
mealsonwheels.org.au
melbourne2006.com.au
ma.org.au (Motocycling Australia)
museumsaustralia.org.au
nationalseniors.com.au
netball.asn.au
probis.com.au
railpage.com.au
rotary.org.au
rspca.org.au
rugby.com.au
reconciliaction.org.au
scouts.com.au
slsa.asn.au
surfingaustralia.com
wwf.org.au
veg-soc.org
zoo.org.au

These days, you can be part of a community without even leaving your house. Joining in is as simple as logging on.

Photo: Sean Murphy / Getty Images

A friend of mine has
never forgotten seeing his
father kiss his grandad's
hand as
he lay in a coma,
just before he died.

It was the only time
he had ever seen
them kiss.

And the only time he
hugged his father was
when his sister died.

It wasn't that they weren't
close, just that they were
grown up,
they were men, and
Australian, and only
death could take down
all the barriers.

But children do it
instinctively – they want
to touch and be touched,
to hold and be held.

So if there was one bit
of advice we'd give
everyone reading this
book, it would be this.

Touch someone you love.

Hold them.

Kiss them.

It's the one piece of magic
we can all do, every day.

Illustration: Tim Ashton

Every year thousands of pairs of specs could be flying to developing countries.

Many of us have old pairs of glasses lying around unused. Yet 200 million people around the world need glasses every year. People who can't see properly can't do their jobs, and kids who can't see properly can't learn at school.

So show some foresight.
Find the nearest place to donate at:
www.optometrist.com.au/donateyouroldglasses.htm

Illustration: Olivia Rayner at illustrationweb.com

Happiness is a fairly traded coffee bean.

When you buy Fairtrade coffee, the small scale farmer who grew the beans is guaranteed a secure future. Fairtrade ensures that the worst effects of the market are avoided by offering a minimum price to farmers that allows them to afford the basics of life – food, shelter, health care and education for their families.

Why is this important? Between 2000 and 2004 most small scale farmers were being paid a 100-year low for their beans – a price well below the cost of production.

We can all ensure that small scale farmers get a fair go by always asking for and buying Fairtrade coffee. If your local supplier doesn't stock Fairtrade coffee ask them to.

Last year Fairtrade coffee sales rose 48% in Britain, 90% in the US and 250% in Australia. Let's keep this trend going and become the fairest country in the world.

www.oxfam.org.au/fairtrade

www.fta.org.au

www.fairtrade.asn.au

Lend a hand on Clean Up Australia Day.

Every year, hundreds of thousands of Australians help clean up their local parks, streets, beaches and waterways on Clean Up Australia Day.

Held every year on the first Sunday in March, all you have to do is visit www.cleanup.com.au to volunteer at a site near you. Then simply turn up on the day with gloves, sturdy shoes, sunglasses and sun protection and sign-in as a volunteer.

We'll guarantee you'll have some good clean fun.

Talk to strangers. Start next door.

Give your phone number to 5 people in your street.

Why not?

They could help you, you could help them, you could make new friends.

My name is:

I'm your neighbour

My phone number is:

Please call if I can help

My name is:

I'm your neighbour

My phone number is:

Please call if I can help

My name is:

I'm your neighbour

My phone number is:

Please call if I can help

My name is:

I'm your neighbour

My phone number is:

Please call if I can help

My name is:

I'm your neighbour

My phone number is:

Please call if I can help

we are what we do

we are what we do

we are what we do

we are what we do

we are what we do

Use of every paper

It's estimated that over 100 million trees are cut down every year for the paper that's used in Australian offices.

So much for the so-called paperless office which everyone was writing all-staff memos about a few years back.

But if we used both sides of the sheet – for instance by pressing the button that says 'use both sides of the paper' on the photocopier – we could halve this.

Let's create a culture in which we make it socially unacceptable to use only one side of paper.

both

sides

piece

of

THIS BOOK BELONGS TO

ACTION 47

BUY A COPY OF THIS BOOK FOR A FRIEND

Isn't this a little bit self-serving, an advertisement for our book in the middle of our book?

But this isn't about making money it's about making change.

For change to really happen at least a million people have to adopt the actions in this book.

So, after you've bought your copy, buy another.

And then give it to the person you think needs it most.
You know the one.

Photo: Paul Schutzer / Time Life / Getty Images

What would you like one million people to do?

One man or woman can change the way we act every day. One such man was Martin Luther King.

Send us your ideas for what you'd like one million people to do, and we'll make them part of the We Are What We Do movement.

wearewhatwedo@pilotlight.org.au

The simple actions in this book are just a beginning.
Discover more from these websites and go further. We are what we do.

1.	LEARN MOUTH TO MOUTH	www.stjohn.org.au www.redcross.org.au
2.	DECLINE PLASTIC BAGS WHENEVER POSSIBLE	www.planetark.com www.cleanup.com.au
3.	READ A STORY WITH A CHILD	www.msreadathon.org.au www.schools.nsw.edu.au/gotoschool/a-z/readingtoyourchild.php
4.	FIT AT LEAST ONE ENERGY-SAVING LIGHT BULB	www.greenhouse.gov.au
5.	SMILE AND SMILE BACK	www.humour.com.au
6.	TAKE PUBLIC TRANSPORT WHEN YOU CAN	www.travelsmart.gov.au
7.	PLANT SOMETHING	www.landcareaustralia.com.au
8.	HAVE A BATH WITH SOMEONE YOU LOVE	www.savewater.com.au
9.	LEARN THE TRADITIONAL OWNERS OF YOUR AREA	www.fatsil.org www.foundingdocs.gov.au
10.	TURN YOUR THERMOSTAT DOWN 1 DEGREE	www.sustainable-energy.vic.gov.au
11.	GET FITTER, FEEL BETTER	www.goforyourlife.vic.gov.au
12.	TURN OFF APPLIANCES AT THE MAINS	www.sustainable-energy.vic.gov.au
13.	RECYCLE YOUR MOBILE PHONE	www.phonerecycling.com.au
14.	SPEND TIME WITH SOMEONE FROM A DIFFERENT GENERATION	www.community.gov.au
15.	REGISTER ONLINE AS AN ORGAN DONOR	www.organdonor.com.au
16.	GIVE YOUR CHANGE TO CHARITY	www.unicef.com.au
17.	TRY WATCHING LESS TV	www.whitedot.org
18.	LEARN TO BE FRIENDLY IN ANOTHER LANGUAGE	www.1-800-translate.com/services/freecomputer/freecompwiz.asp
19.	LEARN ONE GOOD JOKE	www.goodcleanjokes.com
20.	TURN OFF UNNECESSARY LIGHTS	www.www.sustainable-energy.vic.gov.au
21.	FIND OUT HOW YOUR MONEY IS INVESTED	www.eia.org.au
22.	USE YOUR WILL TO GOOD EFFECT	www.law4u.com.au/cgi-bin/factsheet right.asp?article id=492
23.	HAVE MORE MEALS TOGETHER	www.geocities.com/EnchantedForest/Creek/9966/Tabletop.html
24.	DISPOSE OF CIGARETTES APPROPRIATELY	www.cleanup.com.au www.buttsout.net
25.	RECYCLE YOUR CLOTHES	www.ourcommunity.com.au/giving/giving_article.jsp?articled=886
26.	GIVE BLOOD	www.donateblood.com.au
27.	PAY MORE WHEN YOU SHOP AT OP SHOPS	www.communityguide.com.au/community.cfm?/australia cat/clothingfashion/recycledclothing
28.	SEIZE THE MOMENT	www.mgandh.org
29.	RECYCLE YOUR COMPUTER	www.cleanup.com.au/main.asp?RequestType=Doc&DoclD= 189&CatlD=116
30.	BAKE SOMETHING FOR A FRIEND	www.joyofbaking.com aww.ninemsn.com.au/article.aspx?id=27774&subsection name=cookingclass

31.	TURN OFF THE TAP WHILE BRUSHING YOUR TEETH	www.choice.com.au/viewarticleasonepageaspx?id=100228&catId=100285&tid=100008&p=1
32.	BE RESOURCEFUL	www.bunnings.com.au
33.	RECYCLE YOUR BOOKS	www.bookcrossing.com
34.	OFFER TO MOW YOUR NEIGHBOUR'S LAWN	www.volunteeringaustralia.org www.community.gov.au
35.	WRITE TO SOMEONE WHO INSPIRED YOU	www.auspost.com.au
36.	TAKE TIME TO LISTEN	www.depressionnet.com.au www.beyondblue.org.au
37.	DON'T OVERFILL YOUR KETTLE	www.savewater.com.au www.wateraid.org/australia/default.asp
38.	LET AT LEAST ONE CAR IN ON EVERY JOURNEY	www.racv.com.au
39.	SHOP LOCALLY	www.ourcommunity.com.au
40.	JOIN SOMETHING	www.community.gov.au www.wearewhatwedo.org
41.	HUG SOMEONE	www.uta.fi/~ms54336/halia.htm www.onemindonevoice.org/hugs.html
42.	RECYCLE YOUR SPECS	www.optometrist.com.au/donateyouroldglasses.htm
43.	BUY FAIRLY TRADED PRODUCTS	www.betterhealth.vic.gov.au www.global-garden.com.au
44.	CLEAN UP AUSTRALIA DAY	www.cleanup.com.au www.landcare.net.au www.kabq.org.au
45.	GIVE YOUR PHONE NUMBER TO 5 PEOPLE IN YOUR STREET	www.neighbourhoodwatch.com.au
46.	USE BOTH SIDES OF EVERY PIECE OF PAPER	www.recyclingnearyou.com.au www.pneb.com.au
47.	BUY A COPY OF THIS BOOK FOR A FRIEND	www.wearewhatwedo.org
48.	SEND US AN ACTION	www.wearewhatwedo.org
49.	LEARN MORE, DO MORE	www.wearewhatwedo.org www.abc.net.au/spark
50.	DO SOMETHING FOR NOTHING	www.community.gov.au www.volunteeringaustralia.org

We Are What We Do does not receive money from any websites mentioned in this book and is not responsible for their content. If you would like us to add your organisation to the list, please email us at wearewhatwedo@pilotlight.org.au

Many people have contributed to the creation of this book.

We would especially like to thank the following:

IN THE UK:

Illustration Ltd for working with their illustrators to create the images.

Getty Images for collaboration on the photography.

The Book Service (part of the Random House Group) for providing storage and distribution.

Innocence and **ArthurSteenAdamson** for the creation of the We Are What We Do brand.

Wieden + Kennedy for creative support throughout the development of We Are What We Do.

Cathay Pacific for providing travel facilities.

The We Are What We Do team in the UK - **Nick Walker, Sara Smith-Laing, Anne Shewring, Sandra Deeble, Rebecca Leed, Kenn Jordan, Eugenie Harvey and David Robinson.**

Alan Devine
Alun Crockford
Andrew Selby
Andy Hammond
Andy Helme
Andy Holmes
Angus Fowler
Anne Shewring
Ashley Koo
Aurea Carpenter
Bryan Mullennix
Bryn Attewell
Camilla Harrisson
Caroline Mills
Carolyn Francis
Chalkie Davis
Chris Walker
David Day
Ellie Robinson
Gail Greengross
Giles Gibbons
Gray Jolliffe
Graham Pugh
Hailey Phillips
John Lamb
Judy Lambert
Juliette Lott
Karen Baxter
Kate Poland
Kevin Anthony Horgan
Lewis Blackwell
Mark George
Mark Robinson
Mark Williams

Marksteen Adamson
Martin Crockatt
Michael Johnston
Mick Bailey
Mike Reid
Natalie Conn
Nathalie Gelderman
Neil Christie
Nicholla Longley
Nuala Donnelley
Oliver Davies
Olivia Tebutt
Paul Daviz
Paul Schutzer
Peter Eatherley
Poppy Ashton
Rebecca Nicolson
Richard Hoban
Robert Ramsey
Russell Davies
Sara Smith-Laing
Sarah Walker
Shannon Fagan
Sholto Walker
Sophie Hayes
Spencer Jones
Steve Hilton
Stuart Simmons
Sue Souchaud
Tim Ashton
Tony Davidson
Willie Ryan
Zoë Whishaw

Companies:
Antidote
Allen & Overy LLP
Apna Ghar
Brunswick Group
Business in the Community
Channel 4
Community Links
Good Business
Interbrand
Lyndales Solicitors
Royal Mail
Short Books
Three Blind Mice
TimeBank
Time Life
White Door

IN AUSTRALIA:

Pilotlight would like to thank:

All Australian Illustrators and Photographers.

Community Links for inspiring us.

Deloitte for providing accountancy we could count on.

Freehills and our legal eagle **Alice MacDougall.**

Gavin Anderson for their strategic advice with communications.

All the wonderful people at **Hardie Grant Publishing** for their help in sales, marketing and editorial.

Judith Swales & Ricci Swart without whom this book would still be being put together.

Macmillan Distribution Services for providing storage and distribution.

Pacific Brands, in particular **Paul Moore** and **Mary Keely** who helped us when the book was just a dream.

The Joffe Charitable Trust.

Whybin\TBWA for their creative brilliance and seemingly endless patience.

Adrian Lockhart
Alex Fenton
Alex McDonald
Alice MacDougall
Amanda Milledge
Amy Smith
Amy Vale
Andrew Knight
Bettie Kornhauser
Bob Shields
Brian Watson
Bruce Baldwin
Carlos Alcaide
Charles Lane
Christopher Howe
Darren Heveren
David Adams
David Robinson
David Polonsky
Dana Kornhauser
Danielle Roet
Elizabeth Levinson
Ellie Robinson
Eugenie Harvey
Geoffrey Zygier
Graeme Wise
Harry Williams
Ian Smith
Jackie Polonsky
Jane Kneebone
Jane Tewson
Janine Kirk
Jason Eades
Jenny Leeson
Joel Joffe
John Lamanna
John Zelcer
Judith Swales
Kester Brown
Laura Diez
Lauren Oliver
Linda Woolston
Mark Scott
Mary Finnemore
Mary Keely
Melissa Hayes
Michael Hirsh
Michael Syme
Neil Osborne
Nerida Simpson
Nick Diggory
Nick Murray
Nyto Lay
Peta Magick
Peter Kirwan
Paul Hastings
Paul Moore
Phil Martin
Philip Weickhardt
Ricci Swart
Ross Gibb
Sandy Grant
Simon Longstaff
Stanley Harris
Stephanie Exton
Steve Wish
Stuart Crosset
Susannah McFarlane
Veronica Greavrs

Companies:
ANZ Bank
Australia Post
Big Studio
Blue Fish
Community Links
Deloitte
DW Thope
Gavin Anderson
Getty Images
Hardie Grant Publishing
Heaven Pictures
Koorie Heritage Trust
Lyndales Solicitors
Macmillan Distribution Services
Melbourne Cares
Pacific Brands
Pilotlight
The Body Shop
The Pilotlight Board
Whybin\TBWA

and...

...thank you.

If you'd like to show your support, put up your hand.